A Quick Word with

BETH
MOORE

ISBN 978-0-8054-3281-7
B&H Publishing Group
Nashville, Tennessee
www.BHPublishingGroup.com

Unless otherwise noted, all Scripture quotations are taken
from the Holman Christian Standard Bible ® copyright
© 1999, 2000, 2002, 2003 by Holman Bible Publishers.

The other version used is the New International
Version ® copyright © 1973, 1978, 1984 International
Bible Society. Used by permission of Zondervan.

Printed in Singapore
1 2 3 4 5 6 7 12 11 10 09

A Quick Word with

BETH
MOORE

Scriptures & Quotations from
WHEN GODLY PEOPLE
DO UNGODLY THINGS

They conquered him
by the blood of the Lamb
and by the word of their
testimony, for they did
not love their lives in
the face of death.

Revelation 12:11

The more we understand what the covering of Christ's blood means to us, the more we overcome a foe that is otherwise far too strong for us. Satan's worst nightmare is being overcome—particularly by measly mortals.

There is no
soundness in my
body because of Your
indignation; there is
no health in my bones
because of my sin. For
my sins have flooded
over my head; they are
a burden too heavy
for me to bear.

Psalm 38:3–4

Not everyone in a stranglehold of sin is having a good time. Many people who by the grace of God have never been "had" by the devil have no idea of the suffering involved when someone with a genuine heart for God slips from the path.

These things
happened to them as
examples, and they were
written as a warning to
us, on whom the ends
of the ages have come.
Therefore, whoever
thinks he stands must
be careful not to fall!

1 Corinthians 10:11—12

Not unlike the ones
Satan hurled at Christ,
temptations can vary in
type. But one thing is
sure: they are tailor-made
to catch the believer off
guard. Many sincere
believers fall before
they even know
what hit them.

Blessed is the man
who does not condemn
himself by what he
approves. But whoever
doubts stands condemned
if he eats, because his
eating is not from faith,
and everything that is
not from faith is sin.

Romans 14:22—23

If we searched for
the root of our seasons
of sin, we would find
that a disastrous harvest
almost always has its
beginning in a deeply
embedded seed of
distrust. Some level
of unbelief is involved
in every sin.

Everyone who practices
wicked things hates the
light and avoids it, so that
his deeds may not be
exposed. But anyone who
lives by the truth comes
to the light, so that his
works may be shown to
be accomplished
by God.

John 3:20–21

Brick by brick,
God builds a mighty
fortress around our lives
as we learn to bring to
the light (through open
dialogue with Him) that
which we by human
nature leave in
the dark.

May the God of peace
Himself sanctify you
completely. And may your
spirit, soul, and body be
kept sound and blameless
for the coming of our
Lord Jesus Christ. He
who calls you is faithful,
who also will do it.

1 Thessalonians 5:23–24

While all of us have the capability of departing into ungodliness, not all share the same degree of risk. Thankfully, some believers have so wholly allowed their bodies, souls, and spirits to be sanctified, they have a strong defense against seducing spirits.

We proclaim Him, warning and teaching everyone with all wisdom, so that we may present everyone mature in Christ. I labor for this, striving with His strength that works powerfully in me.

Colossians 1:28–29

Satan hopes our horrible experiences will cause us to live in the past. *No way!* This pilgrim is moving forward. But I do keep my experience tucked in my backpack. It serves to warn me along my way and to be of any help to another sojourner.

"Come, let us discuss this," says the Lord. "Though your sins are like scarlet, they will be as white as snow; though they are as red as crimson, they will be like wool."

Isaiah 1:18

Remember, you can't
trust your feelings.
So if you don't "feel"
like you "want" to be
rescued from sinful
behavior, reason with
yourself and admit
that you "need"
to be rescued.

Woe to the earth and
the sea, for the Devil has
come down to you with
great fury, because he
knows he has a
short time.

Revelation 12:12

After catching his prey off guard, the enemy does all he can to make the victim feel completely trapped. But he can't keep up this façade indefinitely.

Since you have been
forewarned, be on your
guard, so that you are not
led away by the error of
the immoral and fall
from your own stability.
But grow in the grace
and knowledge of our
Lord and Savior
Jesus Christ.

2 Peter 3:17–18

Most believers feel invulnerable after a mountaintop experience with God. Actually, that's when we are the *most* vulnerable because falling into sin is the last thing we're expecting. We're wise to expect times of testing after times of blessing.

The weapons of our
warfare are not fleshly,
but are powerful through
God for the demolition of
strongholds. We demolish
arguments and every
high-minded thing that
is raised up against the
knowledge of God, taking
every thought captive to
the obedience of Christ.

2 Corinthians 10:4–5

Breaking free from mentally obsessive strongholds requires bringing those previously exalted imaginations into the captivity of Christ's authority. This is no small challenge—one that the enemy hopes we're not "up to." We have to prove him wrong.

Whenever you turn to
the right or to the left,
your ears will hear this
command behind you:
"This is the way.
Walk in it."

Isaiah 30:21

Sometimes we get a gut feeling that we ought to avoid involvement in a situation, and sometimes that gut feeling is the work of the Holy Spirit.

Let us consider how we
may spur one another on
toward love and good
deeds. Let us not give up
meeting together, as some
are in the habit of doing,
but let us encourage one
another—and all the
more as you see the
Day approaching.

Hebrews 10:24–25 NIV

Satan loves isolation.
He wants to draw us out
of healthy relationships
into isolated, secretive,
unhealthy relationships.
He purposely woos us
away from those who
might openly recognize
Satan's seduction and
call his hand on it.

We know that anyone born of God does not continue to sin; the one who was born of God keeps him safe, and the evil one cannot harm him.

1 John 5:18 NIV

For those who have walked closely with God, the desire for a return to His intimate favor finally exceeds the lure of the seducer. Those who have known the truth will finally recognize the lie.

But you, dear friends,
building yourselves up in
your most holy faith and
praying in the Holy Spirit,
keep yourselves in the
love of God, expecting
the mercy of our Lord
Jesus Christ for
eternal life.

Jude 20–21

Satan cannot
possessively lay hold
on us, keep us in a grip,
or touch us in a way that
will utterly destroy us. We
may "feel" destroyed, but
we are not. Christ will
preserve us from Satan's
ultimate intent—our
total destruction.

If we say, "We have no sin," we are deceiving ourselves, and the truth is not in us. If we confess our sins, He is faithful and righteous to forgive us our sins and to cleanse us from all unrighteousness.

1 John 1:8–9

The sins we commit
in reaction to seduction
and those we commit in
outright rebellion can
be forgiven through the
payment Christ has made
for *all* sins on the cross.
However, we must
approach the throne
of grace *with* truth
and *in* truth.

I am the least
intelligent of men,
and I lack man's ability
to understand. I have
not gained wisdom, and
I have no knowledge
of the Holy One.

We can't just have
knowledge about
warfare to defeat Satan.
We desperately need the
knowledge of God. And
our only means of getting
it is through an intense
relationship with God
through His Word.

I fear that, as the
serpent deceived Eve
by his cunning, your
minds may be corrupted
from a complete and
pure devotion
to Christ.

2 Corinthians 11:3

A head full of biblical knowledge without a heart passionately in love with Christ is terribly dangerous—a stronghold waiting to happen. The head is full, but the heart and soul are still unsatisfied.

Who perceives his
unintentional sins?
Cleanse me from my
hidden faults. Moreover,
keep Your servant from
willful sins; do not let
them rule over me.
Then I will be innocent,
and cleansed from
blatant rebellion.

Psalm 19:12—13

We are so quick to
acknowledge the errors
of others, but one of
our best defenses is to
recognize where *we've*
gone wrong and where
our personal weak places
are. We need to replace
our self-condemnation
with self-discernment.

As high as the heavens
are above the earth, so
great is His faithful love
toward those who fear
Him. As far as the east
is from the west, so far
has He removed our
transgressions from us.

Psalm 103:11—12

God keeps no record
of wrongs, but you can
bet Satan does. He's a
meticulous note taker.
We've got to start
believing God's press
about us and not
the devil's.

Israel, put your
hope in the Lord.
For there is faithful
love with the Lord, and
with Him is redemption
in abundance. And
He will redeem Israel
from all its sins.

Psalm 130:7–8

For thirty years
Satan used my past in
various ways. I finally
began to wake up to the
fact that Satan was going
to use my past until
I allowed God to snatch
it from him and use
it for Himself!

"For I know the
plans I have for you,"
declares the Lord, "plans
to prosper you and not to
harm you, plans to give
you hope and a future."

Jeremiah 29:11 NIV

"For I know the plans I have for you," declares the devil, "plans to totally bankrupt you and to harm you, plans to make you hopeless and to destroy your future."

Strengthen your tired
hands and weakened
knees, and make straight
paths for your feet,
so that what is lame may
not be dislocated, but
healed instead.

Hebrews 12:12–13

God never appoints
us to sin. Even when He
tests His children, His
purpose is to prove godly
character—or the lack
thereof. If a test proves a
lack, God's chief desire is
to enlist the cooperation
of the child and provide
what is lacking.

The Lord said to Satan,
"Have you considered My
servant Job? No one else
on earth is like him, a
man of perfect integrity,
who fears God and turns
away from evil. He still
retains his integrity, even
though you incited Me
against him, to destroy
him without just cause."

Job 2:3

Whenever Satan
turns up the heat,
I often say to myself:
"You have no idea what's
going on out there, old
girl. This could be really
important. Stand firm,
and don't give the yell
leaders of hell anything
to cheer about.
God is *for* you!"

I am sure of
this, that He who
started a good work in
you will carry it on to
completion until the
day of Christ Jesus.

Philippians 1:6

Are you still living?
Then there's still time on
the clock. So get up and
fight! God wants to prove
to the kingdom of hell
that you will prove
faithful.

Simon, Simon, look out! Satan has asked to sift you like wheat. But I have prayed for you that your faith may not fail. And you, when you have turned back, strengthen your brothers.

Luke 22:31–32

Has God permitted
the enemy to launch a
full-scale attack against
you? God knows what
He's doing. He isn't being
mean to you. Maybe this
is the only way He can
get you to attend to
the old so He can do
something new.

Rejoice in the
Lord always. I will
say it again: Rejoice!
Let your graciousness
be known to everyone.
The Lord is near.

Philippians 4:4–5

A primary reason we are
vulnerable to seduction
after we have received the
Spirit of Christ is that we
misunderstand what
we've been given. We
continue to look for
happiness outside
of Christ.

Blessed be the God
and Father of our Lord
Jesus Christ, who has
blessed us with every
spiritual blessing in the
heavens, in Christ.

Ephesians 1:3

In comparison to all we've been given to enjoy in our earthly life with Christ, what we've been called to avoid is like one measly tree in the whole garden.

With every prayer
and request, pray at
all times in the Spirit,
and stay alert in this,
with all perseverance
and intercession for
all the saints.

Ephesians 6:18

A pray-without-ceasing
relationship means seeing
everything against the
backdrop of His presence.
Sometimes saying a lot,
sometimes saying a little,
but living every moment
of life as if He's right
there. After all,
isn't He?

Whatever you do,
in word or in deed, do
everything in the name
of the Lord Jesus, giving
thanks to God the Father
through Him.

Colossians 3:17

If our selfish
hearts are trying to
trick us into feeling a false
sense of dissatisfaction,
a good strong dose of
thanksgiving will cure
what ails us.

Since we are receiving
a kingdom that cannot
be shaken, let us hold on
to grace. By it, we may
serve God acceptably,
with reverence and
awe; for our God is
a consuming fire.

Hebrews 12:28—29

God's is the only fire
that can consume an
object without eventually
destroying it. Anger
destroys. Rage destroys.
Lust destroys. No other
fiery passion in our souls
will ever guard us from
getting burned.

Be sober! Be on the alert! Your adversary the Devil is prowling around like a roaring lion, looking for anyone he can devour. Resist him, firm in the faith.

1 Peter 5:8—9

Do we have to be just eaten up with Jesus? Nope. We don't have to be eaten up with Jesus. We can be eaten up by the roaring lion instead. One or the other is most likely to happen.

The doubter is
like the surging sea,
driven and tossed by the
wind. That person should
not expect to receive
anything from the Lord.
An indecisive man is
unstable in all his ways.

James 1:6–8

We are increasingly surrounded by deception and wickedness. Double-minded Christians aren't going to lose their eternal inheritance, but they are going to be eaten alive on this earth.

As the Father has loved me, I have also loved you. Remain in My love. If you keep My commands you will remain in My love, just as I have kept My Father's commands and remain in His love.

John 15:9–10

I don't think Christ's perfection was the primary guard He had against seduction. His primary guard was that He was totally fulfilled by His Father's love, presence, and will.

I pray not only for these,
but also for those who
believe in Me through
their message. May they
all be one, as You, Father,
are in Me and I am in
You. May they also be one
in Us, so the world may
believe You sent Me.

John 17:20–21

We need one another's prayers desperately. Don't assume that since you've done okay so far without prayer partners, you're not at risk. Commanding us to pray for one another is one of the ways God enforces unity in the body of Christ.

Come and listen,
all who fear God, and
I will tell what He has
done for me. I cried out
to Him with my mouth,
and praise was on
my tongue.

Psalm 66:16—17

Can God do to your
heart what no one else
can do? Can you feel
things with Him you feel
with no one else? Have
you been slain by His
perfect love? Has
He ruined you for
anyone else?

Both the Spirit and
the bride say, "Come!"
Anyone who hears should
say, "Come!" And the one
who is thirsty should
come. Whoever desires
should take the living
water as a gift.

Revelation 22:17

Bride of Christ,
we must never tolerate
a lack of love in our souls
nor let anyone convince
us that it is normal not to
feel love for God. The
Bride was created to
love the Groom.

Listen, Israel:
The Lord our God,
the Lord is One. Love the
Lord your God with all
your heart, with all your
soul, and with all your
strength. These words
that I am giving you
today are to be in
your heart.

Deuteronomy 6:4–6

Seek the real with everything in you. More than life. More than breath. Not just once but over and over for the rest of your days, till your voice is hoarse and with shriveled hand you point to your own aged heart and with one dying word whisper, "More!"

Do everything without
grumbling and arguing, so
that you may be blameless
and pure, children of God
who are faultless in a
crooked and perverted
generation, among whom
you shine like stars
in the world.

Philippians 2:14—15

If we're going to stand firm, we can no longer react. We must pro-act. As the world grows more depraved, the church must grow more alert, more equipped, more sanctified, and much more unified.

Bring charges against me before the Lord and His anointed: Whose ox or donkey have I taken? Whom have I wronged or mistreated? From whose hand have I taken a bribe to overlook something? I will return it to you.

1 Samuel 12:3

Whether we realize
it or not, you and I are
desperate for people who
can see through our lives.
With their help, we can
begin practicing lives of
inside-out veracity that
anybody can see through.

I am no longer in
the world, but they are
in the world, and I am
coming to You. Holy
Father, protect them by
Your name that You have
given Me, so that they
may be one as We
are one.

John 17:11

The last thing we
are going to allow the
enemy to do is talk us
into protecting ourselves
from relationally induced
seduction by shutting our
hearts in a stainless steel
box. Wouldn't that be just
like a bunch of humans to
opt for the easy way out
and detach from people?

No creature is
hidden from Him,
but all things are naked
and exposed to the eyes
of Him to whom we
must give an account.

Hebrews 4:13

God looks upon
all our hearts, and *ours*
must be right before Him
even when we're tempted
to wonder if someone
else's heart is right
before Him.

I have sought
You with all my heart;
don't let me wander from
Your commands. I have
treasured Your word in
my heart so that I may
not sin against You.

Psalm 119:10–11

Do we let the Word of God not just get *to* us but get *through and through* us? If we are not deliberately asking God to get into every part of our business, we're not practicing the approach that will best protect us.

Some of you were like
this; but you were washed,
you were sanctified, you
were justified in the name
of the Lord Jesus Christ
and by the Spirit of
our God.

1 Corinthians 6:11

Satan, the ultimate
Mr. Unclean, hates that
mortal creatures have
been made clean through
the grace of Calvary and
the sanctifying work of
the Holy Spirit. If he can't
make us unclean, he will
at least do everything he
can to make us *feel*
unclean.

Do not be
conformed to this age,
but be transformed by the
renewing of your mind, so
that you may discern what
is the good, pleasing, and
perfect will of God.

Romans 12:2

We can't change
anyone else. We can't
even change ourselves.
But we can allow God to
change us. He can give us
courage to put distance
between us and any
relationship that is a
seduction waiting
to happen.

Many shepherds
have destroyed My
vineyard; they have
trampled My plot
of land. They have
turned My desirable
plot into a desolate
wasteland.

Jeremiah 12:10

Tragically, we often
don't realize part of our
fence is down until Satan
is devouring something
precious to us. Mind you,
the devil has no right to
be on our property, but all
he needs for a written
invitation is a weak
spot in the fence.

How happy is
the one You choose
and bring near to live
in Your courts! We
will be satisfied with the
goodness of Your house,
the holiness of Your
temple.

Psalm 65:4

Too often we live our lives strictly sacrificially. All the fun seems to be outside the walls, and we secretly yearn for something to awaken our souls. But where we are concerned, the grass is never greener on the other side of the fence. It's nothing but artificial coloring.

Again I saw under the
sun that the race is not
to the swift, or the battle
to the strong, or bread to
the wise, or riches to the
discerning, or favor
to the skillful.

Ecclesiastes 9:11

We'd better get a clue.
Life isn't fair. Not from
any direction. I live in the
inconceivable grace of
God every day of my life.
That's not fair either.

I have certainly seen
the oppression of My
people in Egypt; I have
heard their groaning
and have come down
to rescue them.

I think it's possible for some to feel "possessed" by a demon when in reality they are terribly "oppressed." Demonic oppression can be so powerful "on" a person that it can feel "in" the person.

Who may ascend the mountain of the Lord? Who may stand in His holy place? The one who has clean hands and a pure heart, who has not set his mind on what is false, and who has not sworn deceitfully.

Psalm 24:3–4

It is a never-ending challenge to keep our minds clean, and we often grow tired of bothering. But we *must* bother because the mind is the biggest battlefield we have on which our spiritual battles are fought. Even our feelings eventually bow to our thoughts.

Take up the full armor
of God, so that you may
be able to resist in the evil
day, and having prepared
everything, to take your
stand. Stand, therefore,
with truth like a belt
around your waist,
righteousness like
armor on your chest.

Ephesians 6:13–14

Don't let Satan
have another inch.
The first piece of armor
you've got to put back
on is the breastplate of
righteousness. That way,
your injured heart will be
protected by your *doing*
what is right until you
feel what is right.

As for you, because
of the blood of your
covenant, I will release
your prisoners from the
waterless cistern.
Return to a stronghold,
you prisoners who have
hope; today I declare
that I will restore
double to you.

Zechariah 9:11—12

Don't worry about your
future right now. Just
offer Christ your wrist
and tell Him to drag you
home, even if you're not
sure you belong or even
want to go. You do. You
may just be too wounded
right now to feel it.

You were grieved as
God willed, so that you
didn't experience any loss
from us. For godly grief
produces a repentance
not to be regretted and
leading to salvation,
but worldly grief
produces death.

2 Corinthians 7:9–10

If you haven't
already come to this
step, muster up every bit
of the courage you have
within you and ask God
to baptize you in a tide of
sorrow over your sin. Ask
Him to do it for as long
as necessary until full
repentance comes.

I cry aloud to the Lord;
I plead aloud to the Lord
for mercy. I pour out my
complaint before Him;
I reveal my trouble to
Him. Although my spirit
is weak within me,
You know my way.

Psalm 142:1–3

If the Bible is about
anything at all, it is about
God having mercy on the
pitiful plight of men,
forgiving their sins and
restoring their lives.
Christ never resisted the
truly repentant, but the
Pharisees (on the other
hand) could really
get to Him.

My soul, praise
the Lord, and do not
forget all His benefits.
He forgives all your sin;
He heals all your diseases.
He redeems your life
from the Pit; He crowns
you with faithful love
and compassion.

Psalm 103:2–4

God forgives and
forgets because He does
not need to remember.
We are forgiven but do
not forget because we are
wise never to lose sight
of where we've been
and how God has
rescued us.

Now to Him who is able to do above and beyond all that we ask or think—according to the power that works in you—to Him be glory in the church and in Christ Jesus to all generations, forever and ever. Amen.

Ephesians 3:20—21

Our human natures think little of God until we are forced to think more. Ironically, we may need to come to the place where we're desperate enough to consider, "If God is not bigger than I have thus far needed and believed Him to be, I am history."

"Woman, where
are they? Has no one
condemned you?" "No
one, Lord," she answered.
"Neither do I condemn
you," said Jesus. "Go, and
from now on do not
sin any more."

John 8:10–11

I would be nothing
less than a hypocrite if
I refused a brother or
sister the right to draw
from the bottomless well
of God's grace and try
again. I had to learn to
swim in it to live.

Today you have rejected
your God, who saves you
from all your troubles and
afflictions. You said to
Him, "You must set
a king over us."

1 Samuel 10:19

Have you noticed
that big trouble can begin
when we start saying no
to something God has
provided for us and look
for our own more rational
and reasonable means
of provision?

I have set before you
life and death, blessing
and curse. Choose life
so that you and your
descendants may live,
love the Lord your God,
obey Him, and remain
faithful to Him.

Deuteronomy 30:19 — 20

You will either learn
to trust God as never
before, or you will be
impaired the rest of your
life. He will not appoint
any chastisement nor
allow any consequences
that cannot be used *for*
you when all is said
and done.

Everything that belongs
to the world—the lust of
the flesh, the lust of the
eyes, and the pride in
one's lifestyle—is not
from the Father, but
is from the world.

1 John 2:15–16

Our pride will take a beating when we start getting back on track with God, but keep in mind that the sifting of our proud natures is one of God's primary divine intentions. God wants all our pride not only to take a beating but a killing!

Am I now trying to
win the favor of people,
or God? Or am I striving
to please people? If I
were still trying to please
people, I would not be
a slave of Christ.

Bowing to authority
is critically important
and may be a vital part
of the process God uses
to restore you. Still, you
must be careful not to slip
into the trap of seeking
human approval
over God's.

All of us have become like one who is unclean, and all our righteous acts are like filthy rags; we all shrivel up like a leaf, and like the wind our sins sweep us away.

Isaiah 64:6 NIV

If your faith is in your own righteousness, you are in big trouble now. It's time to turn away from all the former things your faith may have been in and trade them in for all the things "the faith" truly concerns.

We know that all
things work together
for the good of those who
love God: those who are
called according to
His purpose.

Romans 8:28

Oh, how God
has used defeats of all
different kinds in my life
for good! There is one
thing I would have hated
worse than some of the
things I've been through
in life: what I would've
been without them.

I have heard the gossip of the multitudes, "Terror is on every side! Report him; let's report him!" Everyone I trusted watches for my fall.

Jeremiah 20:10

We have no business
gossiping about members
of the body of Christ.
If we would turn the time
we spent discussing the
other's life into prayer
time instead, no telling
what could happen to
the glory of God.

As for me, I vow that
I will not sin against the
Lord by ceasing to pray
for you. I will teach
you the good and
right way.

1 Samuel 12:23

You need to know how to proceed from where you are now to where God wants you to go. You need to know the way that is "good and right."

Come out from
among them and be
separate, says the Lord;
do not touch any unclean
thing, and I will welcome
you. I will be a Father to
you, and you will be sons
and daughters to Me,
says the Lord Almighty.

2 Corinthians 6:17 – 18

You've got
to be serious about
restoration. Do whatever
you have to do to cut off
the flow of venom. Get
all the help you need to
make this move and keep
this commitment. It is
a *big* ticket to freedom!

As you have received
Christ Jesus the Lord,
walk in Him, rooted
and built up in Him and
established in the faith,
just as you were taught,
and overflowing with
thankfulness.

Colossians 2:6–7

Doing right is a learned behavior that comes from being taught. We will never cease to be God's children, but when we cease learning and being teachable, we are no longer disciples.

This is how
God showed his love
among us: He sent his
one and only Son into the
world that we might live
through him. This is love:
not that we loved God,
but that he loved us and
sent his Son as an atoning
sacrifice for our sins.

1 John 4:9–10 NIV

God hasn't forgiven us
because our sins were no
big deal. He has forgiven
us because of His great
love. Period. He loves us
so much, He threw all our
transgressions on His
own perfect Son and let
Him die on a cross in our
place. We simply chose
to receive the gift.

If I forget you,
Jerusalem, may my
right hand forget its skill.
May my tongue stick to
the roof of my mouth
if I do not remember
you, if I do not exalt
Jerusalem as my
greatest joy!

Psalm 137:5–6

I'm convinced that the
ability to remember
as if it happened yesterday
is a gift, even though
some days it feels like
a curse. It's worth any
bad memories if
I never forget God's
goodness to me.

No condemnation
now exists for those
in Christ Jesus, because
the Spirit's law of life in
Christ Jesus has set you
free from the law of
sin and of death.

Romans 8:1–2

The accuser says, "Feel
guilty and condemned
for all the great things the
Most High has had to do
for you." Deliberately
refuse to listen to him.
Because the more you
listen, the more
he'll say.

If anyone
purifies himself from
these things, he will be
a special instrument,
set apart, useful to the
Master, prepared for
every good work.

2 Timothy 2:21

Complete restoration is ours—even usefulness in the body of Christ and lives of faithful service. God can work everything together for good and redeem our failures. He will gladly be strong in our weaknesses and show us His gracious favor.

Ground that
has drunk the rain that
has often fallen on it, and
that produces vegetation
useful to those it is
cultivated for, receives
a blessing from God. But
if it produces thorns and
thistles, it is worthless
and about to be cursed.

Hebrews 6:7–8

God can take back
what the enemy stole
from us. But we cannot
persist in doing evil. Just
as a physician says an
antibiotic will not have
its full effectiveness if
not taken under the
prescribed conditions,
God's prescription has
a similar warning.

The report of your
obedience has reached
everyone. Therefore
I rejoice over you. But
I want you to be wise
about what is good,
yet innocent about
what is evil.

Romans 16:19

Cast yourself upon
Him if you don't believe
you can leave a life of sin.
Ask Him to raise up an
army to help defend you
against the enemy. Ask
Him to do whatever
He must do!

I know both how to
have a little, and I know
how to have a lot. In any
and all circumstances I
have learned the secret of
being content—whether
well-fed or hungry,
whether in abundance or
in need. I am able to do
all things through Him
who strengthens me.

Philippians 4:12–13

Feelings of hopelessness
and helplessness come
straight from the enemy.
They are lies. Surrender
yourself now to God,
withholding nothing,
and ask Him to do what
seems impossible to you.
Humble yourself and
receive the help He will
send you as you seek it.

I will praise the Lord
who counsels me—even
at night my conscience
instructs me. I keep the
Lord in mind always.
Because He is at my
right hand, I will
not be shaken.

Psalm 16:7–8

Satan has gotten a lot of
mileage off your guilty
conscience. He doesn't
want to give it up as his
playground. So when he
comes back to accuse, you
are going to have to hold
unswervingly to what
God has told you
in His Word.

Since by the one man's trespass, death reigned through that one man, how much more will those who receive the overflow of grace and the gift of righteousness reign in life through the one man, Jesus Christ.

Romans 5:17

Once we repent of our sins, Christ not only serves as our counselor; He also files the most glorious legal brief in the universe. He declares that all punishment and payment of fines for our crimes have been met.

Out of the same mouth come blessing and cursing. My brothers, these things should not be this way. Does a spring pour out sweet and bitter water from the same opening?

James 3:10—11

Something is wrong
if our coworkers would
be shocked that we go to
church. Most believers
don't work in places
where preaching is part
of their job description,
but would coworkers find
our behavior inconsistent
with our professed belief
system at church?

Who can declare
the Lord's mighty acts
or proclaim all the praise
due Him? How happy
are those who uphold
justice, who practice
righteousness
at all times.

Psalm 106:2—3

God will immeasurably bless your life if you are willing to get real and not act as if you've never been had. In fact, He may grace your future with a greater harvest than your past if you're willing to be real.

We have boldness to
enter the sanctuary
through the blood of
Jesus, by the new and
living way that He has
inaugurated for us,
through the curtain
(that is, His flesh).

Hebrews 10:19–20

Believe what God
has already done for you.
The way has been paved
by the blood of Jesus. The
curtain that separated
man from God has been
ripped from top to
bottom by the tearing of
Jesus' precious flesh.

He erased the
certificate of debt, with
its obligations, that was
against us and opposed to
us, and has taken it out of
the way by nailing it
to the cross.

Colossians 2:14

Tell Him how much
you want to be free of
your load of guilt and
how desperate you are to
receive a clean conscience.
Ask Him to take you back
to the cross where you
first received your
salvation.

If I say to the
wicked man, "You will
surely die," but he then
turns away from his sin
and does what is just and
right—if he gives back
what he took in pledge for
a loan, returns what he
has stolen . . . he will
surely live.

Ezekiel 33:14–15 NIV

The proud will never be free. Humility is pivotal to liberty. Have you done everything you can to make restitution for any wrongdoing? Ask God to show you if anything, no matter how small it seems from human perspective, is still undone.

Rest in God alone, my soul, for my hope comes from Him. He alone is my rock and my salvation, my stronghold; I will not be shaken. My salvation and glory depend on God; my strong rock, my refuge is in God.

Psalm 62:5—7

Many people can
walk beside you on your
road to restoration, but
no one can take you that
last quarter mile to your
Father's arms. No person
can go there but you,
and you will never
be healed until
you do.

You took off your
former way of life, the
old man that is corrupted
by deceitful desires; you
are being renewed in the
spirit of your minds; you
put on the new man, the
one created according
to God's likeness in
righteousness and
purity of the truth.

Ephesians 4:22–24

God desires more
than anything to restore
sexual purity to those
who have been sexually
seduced, but it takes time
to peel away the damaged
character. The pain that
can be involved in the
process demands much
trust in a good and
loving God.

If anyone thinks
he is religious, without
controlling his tongue but
deceiving his heart, his
religion is useless.

James 1:26

Religious position and godliness are not synonymous. Neither guarantees the other. We can be in church leadership positions without ever having a pure and wholehearted devotion to Christ.

Dear friends,
do not believe every
spirit, but test the spirits
to determine if they are
from God, because many
false prophets have gone
out into the world.

1 John 4:1

The last thing I want to do is suggest that we cease trusting people, but be warned that not everyone who appears trustworthy is. Perhaps we've all had times when we weren't terribly trustworthy ourselves.

He was a murderer
from the beginning and
has not stood in the truth,
because there is no truth
in him. When he tells a
lie, he speaks from his
own nature, because
he is a liar and the
father of liars.

John 8:44

Satan targets our
emotions because our
hearts are by their own
nature deceptive. Most
assuredly, where believers
are concerned, the father
of lies is at the heart
of every destructive
emotional tie.

Hear the word of the Lord, all you people of Judah who enter through these gates to worship the Lord. This is what the Lord of Hosts, the God of Israel, says: Correct your ways and your deeds, and I will allow you to live in this place.

Jeremiah 7:2–3

All of us who have been
called to communicate to
the body of Christ must
be cautious to remember
that God doesn't just
want to talk *through* us.
When we cease letting
God speak *to* us, it is
only a matter of time
before He will cease
speaking *through* us.

Restore to me the joy of your salvation and grant me a willing spirit, to sustain me. Then I will teach transgressors your ways, and sinners will turn back to you.

Psalm 51:12–13 NIV

You have complete
biblical permission to
be happy in your faith
and also to do the
unthinkable—be bold
enough to ask *why*
if you're not!

You hide them in
the protection of Your
presence; You conceal
them in a shelter from the
schemes of men, from
quarrelsome tongues.
May the Lord be praised,
for He has wonderfully
shown His faithful
love to me.

Psalm 31:20—21

We are going to have
to find safety in Christ,
hiding ourselves in Him,
no matter what kind
of place surrounds us.
Anywhere He sends us,
He is prepared to
protect us.

Our fathers in Egypt did not grasp the significance of Your wonderful works or remember Your many acts of faithful love; instead, they rebelled by the sea—the Red Sea. Yet He saved them because of His name, to make His power known.

Psalm 106:7—8

The Lord will not reject you no matter what you've done to *your* name. His faithfulness to you is based on *His* great name! His great name stands even if we fall! The Lord will not reject you, child.

Summoning the
crowd along with His
disciples, He said to them,
"If anyone wants to be
My follower, he must
deny himself, take
up his cross, and
follow Me."

Mark 8:34

Let's allow God to
have His unhindered
way with every part of us,
neglecting nothing. As
He accomplishes His
good work, we will grow
increasingly low risk for
defeat and seduction and
increasingly high risk
for joy and harvest.

We are the circumcision,
the ones who serve by the
Spirit of God, boast in
Christ Jesus, and do not
put confidence in the
flesh—although I once
had confidence in
the flesh too.

When you're restored,
if you're truly restored,
you'll be free of the
most seductive yoke
of all—every ounce
of confidence you
have ever had in
your flesh.

If you are pure
and upright, then He
will move even now on
your behalf and restore
the home where your
righteousness dwells.
Then, even if your
beginnings were modest,
your final days will be
full of prosperity.

Job 8:6—7

You will find plenty that
will help you stay right
where you are, but the
compass of your soul is
telling you that you don't
belong there. The only
way out is home.

He got up and went
to his father. But while
the son was still a long
way off, his father saw
him and was filled with
compassion. He ran,
threw his arms around
his neck, and kissed him.

Luke 15:20

Ah, there He is now. Coming across the field. So forget your speeches. Your healing will come in your Abba's tight and passionate embrace. Let Him hold you so close that you can hear His heart pounding from having run to you.